Catherine Young writes from the heart and from the land, with the keen eye of a geologist and the soul of a poet. These are poems in the tradition of Gary Snyder, Mary Oliver, and Louise Glück, poems that honor rural life and the earth itself, poems concerned with the soil, with water, with the changing seasons, and with language. In short, they grapple with what it means to be human and one part of this fragile and natural world.

— Christopher Chambers, editor *Midwest Review*

Geosmin reveals the soil that roots us, the relationships that sustain us, the anger that improves us, the memories that make the future possible. In her compelling new book, poet Catherine Young refuses the solipsism of any language that detaches us from more than human things in order to make us more fully human. Each poem here moves away from complacency, sometimes with a nudge, sometimes a shove.

— Bruce Jennings, Editor of *Minding Nature*, a journal of the Center for Humans and Nature

Worlds within worlds unfold, ambered in words, as we follow her wanderings on the land. Linguistic sensuosity matches the touch of skin on bark, the rocks' dance, time and space openings from trilobite murmurings to the purple shimmer on Lake Superior's shore. We roam through a year of change, visit with dairy and goat farmers in the Driftless region, browse in antique shops, and explore the workings of memory. Young's *Geosmin* envelops us in the sense texture of a region, and distills its perfume.

— Petra Kuppers, author of *Gut Botany*

"In *Geosmin*, the poet, Catherine Young, narrates for readers what it means to unearth the subtle miracles of lichen, streambanks, fossils, and raspberry canes, and in so doing, what it means to be connected to our fragile and dazzling planet."

—Heather Swan, Nelson Institute for Environmental Studies lecturer and author of *A Kinship with Ash*

Geosmin

Catherine Young

Water's Edge Press

Printed in the United States of America

Water's Edge Press LLC
Sheboygan, WI
watersedgepress.com

ISBN: 978-1-952526-09-1

Library of Congress Control Number: 2021949776

Credits:

Excerpt from *Landmarks* by Robert MacFarlane used with the author's permission.

Cover and Section Divider Design: DragonFire Design
Cover image from Unsplash

A WATER'S EDGE PRESS FIRST EDITION

Geosmin

(jee-OZ-min)
from Greek, "earth odor;" the scent of freshly-ploughed soil

Camels in a desert can detect geosmin released from wet ground miles away and track it to find an oasis.

The crucial first step to survival in all organisms is habitat selection.

If you get the right place, everything else is likely to be easier.

—Edward O. Wilson, *Biophilia*, 1984

Elements

Almanac

Heartbreak and Beauty

Of Origins and Aging

Elements

Geosmin

fragrance of soil,
slightly sweet, a kind of jasmine,
with a hint of spice, musky enough
to bring a lover to his knees
and calls to mind

earth, crumbly black, at a warm enough time
for the germination of bean seeds, and
hummingbirds building their tiny nests
while we lie beneath leafing-out trees.

Like the smell of beets, some say.
But I say its essence is far more sweet—
the earthy scent released when raindrops
land on ground, carry the aromatic compounds
of soil creatures and their spores.
Geosmin, essential perfume, leads us to water
when drought and famine are over,
and makes us drink in the scent of rain,
the odor of petrichor. Over millennia
we have been led by our noses.

Geosmin:
found in rock crevice domains,
between mosses and molds,
at the feet of lichen, in caves
of brain folds, a marriage
of rich, dark loam
and love's eternal spark.

Gathering Acorns, Hoarding Words

"...there had been a culling of words concerning nature. Under pressure, Oxford University Press revealed a list of the entries it no longer felt to be relevant to a modern-day childhood. The deletions included *acorn, adder, ash, beech, bluebell, buttercup, catkin, conker, cowslip, cygnet, dandelion, fern, hazel, heather, heron, ivy, kingfisher, lark, mistletoe, nectar, newt, otter, pasture* and *willow*.

The words taking their places in the new edition included *attachment, block-graph, blog, broadband, bulletpoint, celebrity, chatroom, committee, cut-and-paste, MP3 player,* and *voicemail... * For *blackberry,* read *Blackberry*."

from Robert MacFarlane's "The Word Hoard" in *Landmarks*

If children do not know *willow*,
how will they know the scent
of spearmint, or peppermint in cold spring streams,
or how water flow is shaped
by willow root? And if
they do not hear the word *catkin*,
how will they hear the bees
as they forage for *nectar* in willow flowers,
in *hazel* shrubs, birch trees. If children
do not know *acorn*,
how will they play in fall
with the scaly cupule of nut on a finger for a hat,
or plant oak trees
that will outlive them?

How will they see *fern* in wood;
heron, lark, kingfisher, in river, sky, sea;
otter in stream and ocean; *cygnet* in reeds,
and all that dwell beside and among us?
Humankind over millennia has held the world together

with words, a continuous thread woven
through hymns and sagas,
echoed across fjords and geyser fields,
pastures and yards.

And *dandelion*—how will their children,
or their children's children know
the yellow *Helianthus* mirrors of sun
for weaving May crowns,
or launch magnificently silken parachutes?

Lichen

I regret the thought
of burning this club of wood,
this perfect piece
of young maple chosen for our warmth,
its transforming bark
appliquéd frilly seafoam green with lichen,
speckled and peppered with gold.

How many worlds dwell
on one branch of maple?
How many starry sphagnum heads
carpet the stones, and
boulders-not-even-rock, but all
moss-mounded-as-boulder?

I cannot look at lichen on this limb
without empathy. I place it
tenderly back outdoors
as I would a spider cradled in a cloth,
or a moth drawn indoors by light
perhaps seeking the moon,
released, once again,
into night.

Dendrous

If I could not see the window-framed trees,
shapes of leafless umber trunks and limbs
in winter monochrome
I might believe

it is simply an image of my arteries and veins.
If I could not see the flash of sky,
mirroring blue, now silver, I might be convinced

I am river, always calling
from hill to sea, or imagine
I am dendrous water, a creek branching,
gathering liquid and light,
seeking ocean, a deliverer. Or perhaps

I am fir, wood forever
sheathed in resinous green, pulling at sky,
drinking sun even in frozen season.

Rootless, warm-blooded, I lie
beside creek and oak, toes
against stems and stones. I
apologize, I apologize.

Color of Water

Be thou Waters, deep.
> *cerulean, seafoam, steel gray*

Be thou Sky, clear.
> *azuline, cyan, celeste*

Be thou Waters married to Sky.
> *gridelin, pearl, perse*

Be thou Waters raining down.
> *silver*

Be thou Stream, Creek, River.
> *unknowable green; corbeau-shadowed*
> *in growing season; black against snow;*
> *alabaster in deep cold;*
> *ochre, sienna, terra-cotta, tawny, caramel in flood*

> *transparent in hand*

Be thou self, Water, clear and at once, mirror
> *mahogany, viridian*

reflecting all possible color: faces, grasses,
> *gunmetal, gold, slate, amber*

towers, dandelions, mountains, cattails,
seashells, plastic, blood.
> *sanguine*

Be thou arched Veil of Water in sundrenched

     violet–indigo–blue–green–yellow–orange–red

        rain-filled sky.

Be thou Water running
within
and without. Carry away
to the sea
all molecules of earth
made and unmade,

synthesized
and fused from crude
and carbon, and all ideas synaptic.

       iridescent

Be thou Water within each being—
blood-borne,

     incarnadine

chlorophyll-laden—

     verdant

Run through it all, Carrier of Souls and Sand:
sing of life, of death;
       Sing your song of Earth.

Volute

When they walk ancient beaches, cliffs
of layered sandstone, they never seem to understand
that we are the shapes of waves,
that the rhythms of the tides mold all that matters.
They call us fossils without seeing the curl
of the fiddlehead fern, the folds
within each seed and vessel. All of it spirals—
yet not fast enough for them.

They forget the Moon, that conjurer of light, ovum of stone
that draws up the oceans, pulls helix through bone.
They overlook snails as pictographs of waves while shells
coil around the energy of the world. Oceans swell
in all that swirls this volatile möbius path.

All is volute.

Let us watch the Moon rise,
raise tides, turn them over.

Let us witness
the whirling embrace between
orb and ocean, the kiss
as bubbles race upward to hatch.

Stone Circle

You thought stones
are inanimate. Like bones, we carry them
from here to there. We set them
in a ring, and they remain.
But no. Take another look
through your lenses fashioned of silica sand. Rocks
dance when you turn your back to them,
refract colors hummingbirds see
and sing to. While your glass spectacles
dissolve into puddles and reef corals fossilize,
boulders dazzle sky and tree.
They beckon. We haul,
cobble cairns, believing
we mark the passages of planets. All the while
mountains sway and hurl
their molten shimmer to the speed of light.
It's all relative – you, me, the stones.
Listen. Did you really believe
these hills are silent? They are
laughing at our mayfly tempo.
Beauty is stone deep. At what point
do we align our sight
for unimagined changes in hue?

Eloquence Engraved in Stone

"Out of sight in the wood, the creek trickles
its ongoing sentence; from treble to baritone
from dependent clause to interrogative"

from "Description" by Tony Hoagland

Out of sight in the wood, the creek trickles
over broken beaches, fossil shells.
Forgotten ocean, now golden limestone, ghostly swells in

its ongoing sentence; from treble to baritone.
Ancient seas advance, sands heave
against cliff. Trilobite, brachiopod speak

from dependent clause to interrogative;
from certainty to shift. Seas recede, voices quelled,
river bluffs, the layered Midwest hills, emerge carved; treed.

Lost At Sea

Landmarks can vanish in the dark,
bearings lost by night or day
where the heart searches. No moss
can guide the way home
to the north country when snow melts
before it begins. Change is the given—
an endless spinning, and no one
gets to stay for long. Whatever seed-created crystals,
whatever icy sky flashed
water to snow's lattice-work,
the frozen time is gone.
We struggle to hold
ourselves responsible for glacial melt
and sea rise, our mountaintop removals
of Carboniferous realms not connected
to this surprise:

        when fossils
are resurrected and fuel a climate shift,
and no ark arrives.

At a Loss

There is no word
for this waking wonder of day
that never ends, even in dark
where the creek lets out as endless line
its liquid canon

a song that goes on
through the facies
whether rock
or not.

If we take down these hills,
crush and slam frac sand deep against shale
there is no word to tell
how these lands shone with corn,
with bone of mastodon
or crystalline stone,
and once rolled as waves in ocean.

When I wake
I have no word
for the shifting soil
singing beneath
the soles of my feet—
even Thanks seems so fleet.

I have only the words spoken
before sunrise—
before *migizi* has flown:

Good Morning.

Shepherd of Trees

What would you trees have of me today? Can I provide you
with heat or shelter? Can my limbs bring you sweet fruit in
summer's golden time? When late winter comes, do you
need songs sung to remember the waking mycorrhizae; of
phloem filling with sap? Do you need a reminder of green,
that you will have green again around you, held by you,
that beneath the thick bark that wraps you, your living layer
is green and sleeps in its own verdancy? If I give you a field,
would you claim it a wood, filling squared-off space until
you grow right through fences? Do you want my easily
abraded skin to wrap around you, comfort you with its
branching capillaries, warm your frozen bark? Be comforted.
I move among you, my feet seeking tendrils.

Almanac

Firefly Nights

June,
stay a while. Linger
with me until the last
bloom on the basswood tree
withers, and the bees move on
to bergamot. I'll see you
in the jars of cherry jam,
the memories of first potatoes
and toes in cold lake waters.
And later, in December, when it's hard
to remember what is now or real,
when I look to the night sky above
the frosted field to seek
Orion's steady guidance, I will hold
the afterimage of sparks in the night
above each creek and stream:
arteries of fireflies, glittering rivers of light.

Midsummer

Midsummer's morning musk
permeates every atom, scented
like birch-smoke and melted beeswax
soaked into the wood of a restored cabin brought over
from Norway, or honey-sweetened Swiss biscuits,
tierggel, golden dough rolled and pressed
in woodcarved forms, encrypted with raised messages,
baked words of wisdom from other times.
Today, the bee-scent draws me to see
the basswood tree flowering at the creeks' edge,
the clover in field calling the swarm in my bone
to rise, to decipher
the ancient code of nectar.

July 4

Summer-baked, parade-ready we stand, hands
in pockets or on cameras. We talk
askance, neighbor-to-neighbor always
about the weather
and whether any of us will make that window of sunshine
to dry our mown hay, and if the least of us
will throw in the towel.

We are a ragged lineup, Midwest
plump and unafraid to show ourselves
in shorts and T-shirts. Propped up
in thick-soled sneakers along our small town street
we are all, or will be, or have been
4-H moms and dads, 4-H
everyone gathered who has ever lived here in this
muddy little bottomland.

From the outside, our tableau
looks like democracy a là Norman Rockwell, only
more cornfed. Even our sheriff's deputy
has equal footing as she waits at the blockade.

We hold two hopes to be self-evident:
as soon as we can, to march from blazing sun
toward picnic shade and cold beer,
and, at next year's parade,
to find one another still –
against all odds – standing here.

Sweet Land of Liberty

At Devil's Lake, the busiest state park in Wisconsin
on the Fourth of July, a place I would never go,
and never at this peak time but for a reunion with ex-pats,
the long line of cars entering along Park Road
is at a standstill, like the bathroom lines where
we strangers chat as we stand waiting, part
of a summer picnic tapestry. Clusters of families
dot the beach lawn in shade and sun, grilling
a million meals. Languages from every continent
coo to babies in strollers, laugh as frisbees fly, and I
am at home in my country, this America,
the diverse place I cannot see
from my farm kitchen window.
High above the lake, I trudge the rocky trails.
Hives of families climb, apologize
in an array of accents when I step aside
to let them pass. I am surprised
by their humble politeness, as if I am not
just another American born of immigrants.
Back down at the bottom,
the lines at the broken bathrooms wrap
around the building while mothers merge to help
each other's children take a drink of clean water,
reassure them all that we're safe together.
In our group around the picnic blanket, we are
world travelers. I ask one who has been to Turkey,
Iran, Turkmenistan, if she feels safe
in those places. She assures me she does. She tells me

People everywhere are so much alike
and want the same thing: to have picnics together with their families.

On this day of celebrating our nation
I wonder where our elected officials
have taken their picnics, and if
they believe in the gatherings of families in public places.
For one day, I am in the real America, a place
where everyone can freely play together as everything crumbles.

Shoreline Instructions for Lake Superior

1. Saunter Superior's shore. Contrast water against sky.
In your mind's eye drop the perpendicular of balsam fir
to basalt ledge as you listen to The Voice in the Lake.
Draw sine waves of sound within.

2. Dig at the purple shimmer place where water meets sand.
Reach for stones, smooth and white as turtle eggs.
Pluck agates the colors of lake tankers, rust and black.
Pick ones that call to you. Rub your fingers
over their sleek surfaces. Pocket the ones which choose you.

3. Prepare to cross the liminal; give over to frigid.
Slide your feet in the cold wet sand.

4. Without hesitation, before it's too late, immerse yourself.

5. Return to the sun-heated shore.
Shake sand from towel and shoes, but not your heart.
Keep a few grains until next summer.

Superior

It is the rare summer day of a northern Great Lake.
Two moms and three kids sit rocking in waves
on the far shore of Madeleine Island. Lake Superior calls
a blue horizon against salmon sands, chants
a song of slap and shush against children's joyous shrieks.
Barefoot gray-haired elders – who elsewhere
would be strangers –
immerse in lawn chairs, soak their toes,
sit in as relatives for the day, presiding
over an afternoon of sand mirrors, slapping feet,
drip-castle villages and whisperings
of other summers' children
while one mother, toweling her daughter tells her
You will travel the world someday, yet this day,
this place, is right at the top.

Waters, Silvered

Waters silvered by cirrus sky and summer's high sun
drive rollers shoreward to us on rust-colored sand. Our hands

plow cold waters, our feet sweep the line between sky
and land. For a while we imagine that summer

goes on forever, that unyielding water, firn beaches
in frozen season, are mirage. Instead, water

envelops us always, and always a breeze arrives
at midday, when rising waves rock and lap

our deepest core and gulls suspend, wings spread
timeless, as if painted there, above ocean shore.

Rime

We met long ago at the inland sea—
lazed and swam Superior's copper shore,
rode island ferries shouting poetry,
singing above the massive engines' roar.
We packed raspberries into cordial wines,
ruby gems bright against boreal land,
saving colored jewels for harder times:
autumn, farewells, and snow on frozen sand.

How could we imagine years passing, when
sailing the broad curving spiral of time,
that we might emerge as gray-haired women?
But we meet again, surprised. All the rime
crystallizes, magnifies who we've been:
the girls on summer's shore when young and prime.

Elderberries

Black Elderberry (*Sambucus nigra*, spp. *canadensis*) known for its culinary and medicinal uses throughout the world, is known by many different names: Elder, Fläder, Sureau, Sambucus, Sambuci, Sauco, Hollunder, Ellhorn…

Collect them, my elders told me.
When they are ripe, cook them into preserves
or syrup. Do not eat them uncooked.
They are medicine to keep you safe, to keep you
from illness and coughs, to keep you breathing
through the worst times. You can eat them,
but you must prepare them first. For some, raw,
straight from the stems, elderberries are poison.

I plucked and tasted them anyway,
surviving their dark seedy bitterness,
worth the effort and stains on the hands,
because they held the flavor of wild
and were available for the taking.

But now, late August, elderberries ripening
are the taste of my daughter leaving home for college,
of darkness on the tongue ripped vivid pink from the inside,
the color of a wound, bull's-eyed by Mercurochrome—
the color of danger. The tongue wants to shout,
Watch out!

These are words unspoken. I find no way
to separate from the rawness of this time,
nor the seed from flesh in the ripening.

Stippled Passing

You could see the gilding beneath
those stippling waters, the speckles
of a trout's back, sleek
and slipping along golden gravel,
shadowed streambanks; among
grassy striations of summer's heat
passing.

You may have wanted eternal summer—
that moment so perfect with mint-lined streams, trees
unwilling to give up their green.
But if time stood still, sun in brassy sky
steadily beaming, you would turn, seek the shift
to bronze, to that time of deciduous rain.
You would seek crimson's run, fill baskets
with round, sweet apples,
and let the pigments of the roseate world drain.

Let be. Release your hold on the season.
You may no longer see the gold
purled beneath the rippled stream. Gold in water
is fleeting flash: memory's afterimage. Creek waters
and sun roll on. Hidden along the stream's ledge,
trout sleep, dream.

As We Wait for Winter

On our farm,
last fresh apples and red cabbages
fill the fridge in pails.
Brussels sprouts and reptilian Nero kale,
dark green against golden hay mulch,
holding on so long against deep-freeze,
offer themselves up.
Within days, fried butternut squash
replaces apple on the daily menu.
Two randy goat bucks penned
beside the does
plead for mercy.
We dress two turkeys.
November's light
bids us to stash sweets.
Woodpile grows,
box elder beetles creep
indoors, and for three consecutive nights
we usher a small brown bat from our house,
open the door to the sepiaed world,
and release her.
Then, snow drifts in,
covers field now glowing
beneath a waxing gibbous moon.
Against the bluing cold,
farmhouse windows shine gold
from light within.

The Ripening Abecedarian

And every good thing comes to an end:
butterflies seal up the chrysalis and sigh while
cherries await sun's heart to release their
dark fragrance to the sky, call orioles to take and
eat each berry, carry each across field to shadowed
fencerows, deposit spoils in sheltered
ground. Yet, ripening is not an end. Fruits carried to
hidden places conspire—they plot and scheme to
invest their reach. Peaches, pears, raspberries'
juiciness invites the same—a game of sorts, in parched July,
kindling avian desire, the flash of jeweled color
    hitches a ride in beauty's beak.

Look to the ripening.
Make promises to an unknown. Move deeper in time. Send
notes to dreamers and orchard growers to pluck each
offering; to sort and toss, sowing windfalls,
proffering nectar's possibility. New generations spark
quietly in Earth's electric heart. Quickened by ferment,
ripened to rot, sweet flesh vanishes. Caterpillars dissolve.
Softened presences merge in
time's fertile womb. Pits and kernels disrobe. Decomposed,
undone, they lodge in soil, and like pupae, re-form; reveal
verdancy. Cotyledons unfurl. Rhizomes spread; affix.
    Stems and roots reach;
wet, veined wings emerge from the clear-shelled chrysalis.
X-ing spirals of down and up, stalk, blossom, and insect
yield to sun's exquisite kiss. Butterfly tongues
    sip new season while summer's memory ripens in
zymurgy's elixirs.

Winter-Laced Lovesong

Like a snowshoe's golden ash heartwood
lashed and woven with hart sinew
I will bear you through the fiercest storms,
carve a path through
many winter's histories. Let me
bend my shape to yours,
flexible in long journeys.
Survival's net is laced with stars
and framed by honeycombed portals,
hexagonal, echoing
snow's ephemeral crystals,
that, like my love, grow
endlessly anew.

Minus Forty

In extreme cold
thermometer becomes icon
at dawn, dusk, and times in-between.
Water becomes a source
of amazement. How, in the house, it flows, mellow
until mercury drops, then bursts pipes forged in foundries.
Pale needles grow beneath dead grasses,
frost ferns and trees flourish on windows
unleashed like some tropical forest.
But this is not the equator, nor the tropics:
it is a place of glass—that slow liquid
our eyes cannot trace, and while we seek clarity
crystals grow all around us.

Stoke the wood stove. Turn up the thermostat.
While creaks and crackings begin, huddle.
All you need
is to keep alive
one
fluid
green
thought.

January Brink

Strange how, standing in my thickest winter parka
in our snow-covered field, I have no insulation
from January sadness—not the longing for summer's green
growing, water free-flowing, late nights of light,
elegant foods, of languid gathering. Instead,
I mourn winter's passing. Fallen flakes will aggregate
to corn snow (who knows why it's called that)
and in mere weeks, amber grass blades will re-inflate
with green. If my life traverses the path of lemniscate—
the figure-eight pattern of daylength
on a mathematician's graph—
solstice extremes of light and dark are the year's
outer reaches, and January
is where cliffs meet sea on the far banks
of some Scottish island, where all we can do
is turn back, cross the middle of deep
and fling ourselves to the other side
not knowing, or remembering,
if the fullness of June is so much better than this:
midday January,
clear sky,
sun-drenched snow
where my tracks
across the new year's field
pool blue.

Late Winter in Dieter Hollow

Like wool strands drawn by hand
from roving readied for the drop spindle,
wind pulls steam from the spring creek
as the stream's relative cold meets
frigid air.

On the ground, snow is lithic,
blizzard followed by rain, then

more cold in extreme.

Deer become bold, browse
every last raspberry cane and apple branch
within reach. Skunks rouse,
leave tracks in snow like cat feet.

In our farmhouse we drowse,
consume pies and Dutch oven beans.
And though bitter cold stretches as far
as we can see, and laundry
still freezes into thin boards, light begins
its opening march. I am willing now

to concede the release
of the frozen world to melt,
and, being practical, to wish it
to melt
without speed.

In February It Begins

All it takes
is the drop that slips
along the glassy slope
of icicle. Maples on the hillside
nod, imperceptibly. Robins
descend upon hackberry fruit
while snow searches its crystalline memory—
remembers something about melt:
beaded water, strung
and running down—
hillside woods and duff
let go of ice,
snow.

Echoing the downy woodpecker's tap,
my child's hands, surrounded by his father's,
place the spile for maple sap.

Verdancy

1

Amid bare umber trunks and branches
the eternal moss and verdigris-covered cliff crouches,
a beacon.

2

Emerald – the color best for our eyes – rises, re-inflates
each grass blade, animates
while we wake, eat, sleep.

3

Fields convert viridian.
Woodlands hold back.

4

Trees become rivers channeling sky to earth, wet
to verdant unfurling.

5

Buds burst, cast off sheathes, reveal prasine.

6

Willows flare gold to green while
trilling, trilling April stirs.

Hymenoptera I: Wasps

My sisters of tiny waists
and hooked wing;
of crane-like legs trailing thoughtlessly
behind, you cling to eaves,
mandibles able to deconstruct
my house while you build anew each year.
I wonder what drives you to tear
and vibrate, plaster a paper lantern nest
so perfectly placed to shed bitter weathers; your cone
is shaped with spiraled intentions
for your brood. So much
work in a season, fierce
purpose. I fear you, your sting, your hum,
that ferocious roar of sisterhood.

Let me not harm you, sisters. My heart's
desire for sanctuary is like yours: encircled
by this humming, this
home building, layer by layer
from the grit and spit
of the world.

Heartbreak and Beauty

Aubade for the Never-Ending Flow of Milk

There were the days of goats, and goats,
and milking our Nubian goats, holding them in place
to help their kids latch, *Come on latch!* while we
praised them, stroked their noses
and long, lovely ears.

There were the sleepless nights
of rising to the call of a kid caught in a fence
or the pleading calls of our does
frightened by predators, sounding for all the world
like abandoned elders in a nursing home,
or the murmured call of the buck professing his love
throughout the neighborhood
from his separate pasture across the road.

There were nights our children dozed deep,
dreaming the sleep of the milk-sated
while we, in freezing February waited and waited
for another kid to drop, needing our help—
and the next milking at dawn.

Invocation: Call It Home

To this place,
Wisconsin, *the gathering of waters,*
we bind ourselves, call it home.

Through seasons droughty and wild we marvel
at our inability to tame weathers
or waters. We cannot leave the river. When she roars
we call her fickle, follow her trail of flotsam
just the same as stumping behind
a maladjusted baler flinging hay
beyond the rick: we pick up what's tossed
only to come back and try again.

Like caddis fly larvae in spring creeks, cobbling homes
of gravel and spit, hunkering in cold and wet, we wait
for that ripe glorious May afternoon
to soar.

We are does listening for danger, watching
for the swing of the antlers that lift
and set us in flight.

Coyotes howl at the edges, hungry
for spoils we won't share:
our caches of dried morels, flagons of maple syrup.
Ours is a king's lair.

We call this land home because we are here.

We wish for nothing more
than pie in summer,
peenting woodcocks in spring, soaring
over fields where turkeys fan,
gravy in fall,
wood-fired winters.

We too, smell the changes seasons bring and still, we stay.

Therefore,
let us bless these streams with rod and creel;
these fields with trowel and seed. Fill
our bellies with berry and cream and brim
our hearts full.

What I Love About Where I Live, Driftless Region

The missing glacial remains, making its name sound
as if it is unshackled; unanchored; unconstrained.

Rounded hills with their straight-lined limestone hearts.
I pretend they are mountains.

Waters seeping from every crevice—clean, constant,
comforting as it sings, threading its way
to the Mississippi River.

All of the bright-green growing world rich in wild foods
to feed a pemmican heart with blackcaps and hickory nuts,
and wild apples from trees planted by deer.

Alphabet-lettered county highways passing
former dairy farms and the crossroads where
cheese factories once stood.

Golden gravel township roads that sing to my child-heart
of Yellow Brick Road; handcrafted houses nestled
against hills with their dreams, so innocent.

The librarian in Solar Town whose two-story palace
contains a coffee maker and glass elevator,
and she'll take you on a ride to the second floor.

The mail carrier, who still tethers each of us
to one another, weaving a township
from which most of the people have departed.

The snows, when they come, deep and thick to receive
my wooden skis; maple sap in buckets shining blue,
and on a clear winter day, the blue flames
from each step in snow; redwings and peepers in March;
snap peas in June straight from the vine; barn swallows
swerving in July; sandhill cranes passing through;
goldfinch and chickadee song all year, but especially

the way the light angles between these creek-carved hills,
each day of each year of all the decades I have lived here.

Art Goes Unbidden

Art goes unbidden
among my rural neighbors, the ones
who have always been
here. Strange ideas come
from those who've never left
their home place,
who wish to make their mark—
the man who tries
to arrange his woodpile
so the logs of dark
red elms spell out his name
amid lighter splits
of ash and oak.

Uncalled for, art shows up.

Each In Their Own Time

"Each in their own time settled deeper"

from "Almanac" by Lois Parker Edstrom

On the farm,
we settle deeper each year
into debt
and soil. What binds us here
but gravity and endless
circling seasons
that wind
tighter
like a watch spring being wound
or
like the turns taken round each
labyrinth bend when walking the path
to its petaled center,
this knowing each year:
the first honeybee's flight,
the swallows' return and departure;
breaking ice on the livestock tank, waiting
for rivulets beneath the road's frozen skin.

We forgot long ago
how it all begins, this ride
so caught in troubled
love of land. We cycle
like sun-drawn waters' rise
to a humid August sky,
and fall surprised, hard,
like December's frozen rain
covering what remains undone.

When Freshly Painted

In the canvas of my memory
it is May, the bulb-sprung flowers
full in bloom—
the rain-washed air, soft. I hear
the breeze, the rooster's scratching feet,
the red hens' startled squawks
as they race away from each egg laid hidden.
And I see you there, husband,
lean, lifting yourself to the seat of the tractor,
your hair still gold, its waves catching spring's
showering light, mirroring sun and shadow
on furrows spread before you, prescience
of light's sparks on corn rows in mid-July.
No dark glaze lies concealed beneath this scene. Instead,

like porcelain figurines, the red hens are perfectly placed,
tipped, tails in air as they peck grit, as we ready
the fields of our lives, straight-lined with every hope
to the vanishing point, that time for us when
all was new,
no distance too great,
and our hearts: cottage doors
freshly painted.

In the Time of Climate Change

When the rains came down
we sighed with relief for the parched soil
and shriveled corn, a belief in water's return:
the creek again full of song.

When the rains came down
we slipped on muddied roads
and farmyard muck,
crossed trenches, overflowed
as we looked for sun—

But drenching rains came until
everywhere puddles shone.
Water pounded windows and walls.
Hillside slopes sprouted waterfalls.
Creeks filled, yards slickened.

Waters rose; roads submerged.
In cornfields, floated fence posts emerged
while livestock, bathed in flood's silt,
struggled to stand: sinking, stinking, sickened

when the rains came down.

Farmer / Janus

Never thought I'd see the day
when I could let it all go, cows
in their stanchions, hay
in the mow, swallows'
cupped-mud nests clinging fast.

Empty at last
the barn sings of wind, ghosts, horses,
curses. I find my way
home from a factory at night,
my barn dark. Now?
No regret:
no livestock to feed,
no manure to haul, no need
to worry, and yet

I am unnerved. I cannot
repay my debt
to this beautiful dirt.

The Shots Came Quick

From the creek brush at the bottom of the hillside field,
the shots came quick.
One dropped, then the other—
doe, then buck, both yearling deer
from the many sets of twin fawns last summer,
both from the herd that plagued our orchard and crops.
The hunter caught them swift, mid-leap;
shots true and clear in intention.
One full-grown doe I have seen before
descended the far end of the field alert; on edge;
and catching the scent of wrong,
she vanished.

So many years I have watched
the fawns, the yearlings, the heavy-shouldered bucks
parade field and yard. I have watched their increase
following the death of farms here; seen their young born
in the woodlot edge graze where dairy cows once stood.
I cannot begrudge them their due from this land
so altered and confused; neither wild nor tame. Mostly,
I cannot blame my neighbor, the hunter—once a farmer—
who, with his child, needs the food.

I pull forelegs; the hunter hind.
We slide the bodies along November grasses
satisfied. The deer lived a good life.
Like us, they ate of wild
and tame, and as I would wish,
dropped with the beauty
in their eyes of trees and sky—
and sky.

Barn Elegiac

Ninety years of squab in the cupola,
mud fonts fashioned by swallows line the beams.
Halters, tines of hand-set rakes
hold the dust of decades.
Scattered straw carries the memories
of long-dead horses buried with the calves.

In brighter days, gambrels and glory adorned oaken boards
coated with red oxide and rye paint. This barn
withstood storms, tethered strength and shelter
with pulse of heifers, Percherons' muscle and mind,
meadow-sweet breath of Golden Guernseys,
filled milk cans, felines prancing along rafters,
all the unnamable creatures of the ever composting.
The beings of this barn warmed its walls; their breaths
infused each beam and board,
and like invisible integument, kept it upright

until,
one snowy night, freed of the living warmth
of even one dung beetle,
down, it comes—
chestnut timbers prostrate beneath
corrugated roof, cedar shakes.

In the end, after the fall,
the scavenged red-painted boards, aged and faded,
are gathered, cut, and hammered
to a vacationer's bedroom wall.

Compost

We buried our Nubian goat buck
at the base of the compost pile,
beneath soiled hay from the barn
containing last spring's stillborns
now decayed.
He was beautiful, that buck, at ease
with his pasture. Each September
we listened as he declared *love*
in the night air. It rolled across the bottomland,
a gentled trumpeting, softened, for does' ears.
Now his offspring,
wethers and one young buck,
walk around the compost pile, graze on
what weeds they find above snows
until a new season brings
green pastures' return in spring.

For Those Who Thought They Could Buy a Farm

Listen:

Did you know that next to your
renovated dairy barn residence,
your *Better Homes and Gardens* mansion
stands out just a little bit from
the rest of this run-down
neighborhood? I mean, your SUVs
don't even carry the local dust
from our lonely roads. You must
wash them pretty often. Did you know
that there are those of us
who roam the road in September
for puffball mushrooms, bigger than
a round loaf of your favorite
artisan bread?

Listen:

There are those of us who belong here
in this place scribed by contoured corn,
hay strips, and curving woodlots. We are
a little different from someone who
never knew a corn picker from a baler.
Oh, we swagger as we twang
our yeah-no responses to each other's stories,
shootin' the breeze, standing along
rusted barbed wire still strung between
our eighty-acre rectangles. The breeze
now mostly wafts above fields overgrown with weeds,
over woods that used to be pastured when the air
was dairy, scented with cow and cheddar.

Staying where we belong means we sink into
an impossible mortgage, settle
in a farmhouse mostly unchanged over fifty years
while barns degrade or go down;
we raise feeder calves
and go to work at a factory far away
in some town.

Your words, though kind,
have no meaning here.
We belong, because we tried
to make it work once,
in rural America. We farmed.

Of Origins and Aging

In Dark Times We Gather Light

In my childhood I breathed the work of bees.

The holy fragrance of burning beeswax scented the air
of the chapel where nuns knelt. Smoky essence of honey
embraced their clustered forms. Habit-clad
in black gown and veil, they raised their faces
in prayer. Their white wimples caught and reflected
veils of jeweled light from stained glass.
I remember the nuns

and weep at the sight
of the statue beside the empty one-room school—
a Franciscan sister sculpted in bronze; a young nun,
ringing the school bell, calling ghost children together,
her wind-swept garments frozen in time.

> Sisters, striped black and white, cloistered
> and clustered and kind, Where have you gone?

Thinking of sisters
in the deepening dark of November
I melt beeswax in my kitchen, remembering
our honeybees, our *apis* sisters who create comb,
shape their cellular cathedrals from veils
of gathered sunlight. Hexagonal chambers of glory,
of gold, dissolve before me in my kettle.

When I last saw our bees alive,
they chewed open the wax portal of the hive—
a sudden shift from warm spring day, to sub-zero.
Too early for their first forage (dandelion, willow)
honeybees rose. Too early in March light

they took flight. Deep cold returned; I saw them
no more. Inside the opened hive in May, they lay
strewn, all dead.

Brushing dead bees from honey-filled combs,
mourning bees, I watch their cathedrals dissolve;
I skim wax; pour molten gold; send gratitude
for light gathered and transformed. I save wax
to melt into healing balm.

We dress in white for St. Lucia Day,
the Swedish celebration of light at winter solstice,
place beeswax candles on Lucia's golden crown
and into the hand of each child as we process
through school halls. We bring breath of song
to darkened classrooms; light from candles recast
from beeswax gathered in churches,
beeswax bearing prayers; holding sweetness;
offering hope.

> *Oh Sisters All, still in dark times*
> *we light candles made and remade, like*
> *stone reshaped into sand; water to snow.*
> *From your work, Sisters, we make*
> *and remake possibility*
> *gathered from luminescence.*

> Spring unfolds again. Draperies of birdsong
> flutter down, from robins
> to cardinals

to doves.
From daffodils
to tulips
to lilac,
color and fragrance will blossom, partnering
with early flowers of tree and field, calling bees,
scarce in our farmyard now,
but on this day, errant honeybees,
bumblebees, come to me

as I sit in my bright yellow coat. They ask,
are you a dandelion in bloom? Or perhaps
a willow inflorescence?

No, I tell them. *I am not what you seek.*

Or maybe I am.

Maybe I wish
to be nectar droplets
consecrated by canticle of mourning dove;
collected and carried in bee belly;
disgorged in hive; fanned over; concentrated
into powerful salve of sunshine—
the honeyed smear of blooming life
prepared to seal out darkness; ready
to heal.

Baptism

Beyond the placards of words
that cover the first grade varnished desk,

    this   that
    he she it
       is   are
    was   were

two syllables float into view:

        ri ver

    You speak them.

Teacher smiles and nods and all at once
you can see, *yes!*
the stream of words
as it joins another
        and another

and the waters rise—
they rise, *yes!*
and you hear rapids
while your lips
push out words
 cascading
       sweeping you
down one torrent
     to another
      surging
       as current
        courses through you

words pour,
        propel you forward :

you shiver as the spray hits—

        sweeps you   away

    Your desk becomes a gleaming wood canoe
        and just as you wonder how you'll
            steer this craft

Teacher holds out your paddle

           you plunge it in
              dip and pull
           S stroke
           J stroke
           feather forward
              dip and pull

           for a moment
           you turn

           back, raise your paddle
           in salute to

Teacher
as she waves
from the
far
far
shore.

Purple Lines

I loved those times in elementary school
when the teacher handed out mimeographed papers, designs
fragrant with ink, lilac-colored outlines, images
for the school year's iconic calendar.
There was something sweet about the scent
and how the world fell neatly within
ropes of spring-crocus lavender, shaped
just enough to suggest form,
not too constraining, or demanding, but kind. I imagine
a microscope looking into my heart could still find
the outlines etched for each month's celebration:
September's autumn leaves; maple, beech, oak leading
to October's jack-o'-lanterns; November's cornucopia,
a plenty we never had, but loved to fill in;
December's candy canes on conical evergreens;
February's cardioid drawings for cut-out valentines.

In my childhood, in the land of coal mines, colors beyond
black, ash, and rust only existed for us
in the palette of wax crayons, hues
found in an eight-piece box. The world
was sketched simpler then, in those times—
as it always has been for children. We learned our shapes,
our primary colors, our timeline of seasons. We knew
what was proper as we sat with mimeographed reasons
for art. But we dreamed; pushed our colors
to the edges, when our part was simply
to stay within purple lines.

Poems Appear Like Light

like sunlight sifting through trees,
a shimmer on forest duff—

> and all at once, you see the opening,
> an invitation to follow
> like Alice chasing after her rabbit—

Run
> to the shine you've sought all your life: the trail left off
> when your mother called you home for chicken soup;
> when your children call you back to them—

> Slip away, try again
> > to climb the holy slant of light thrown from a rift
> > in overcast sky, or ascend twilight's frothy pink frills,
> > the alpine mirage shining above hills,
> > clouds mounded on horizon—

> Reach again
> > for coral rays, a distant vision, the edge
> > between imagined mountain and heaven, but
> > tumble, feel the thud of your arms and knees
> > on grass as you land.

> > One more time make a pass
> > > for light,
> > > sweep your hands through the aria
> > > of descending night
> > > as fireflies glimmer, and rise.

Letter to the Fifteen-Year-Old Artist: On Wishing

Oh dear one,

    As you look out the classroom window on your
decaying city, you try to do what your high school English
teacher has asked. In this thinning light of fall, leaves drop,
expose naked branches, framing your city's skyline.
You try to imagine other lives though you do not know
what the light looks like through branches on streets
in a city that is not yours.

    At fifteen, you wish for love,
and it's around the bend, seeking you—
a sweet one whose nearness will make you tingle.
You will know love, loss, and your wishes

will fill like an expanding sponge
in a glass bowl of water, though you
believe, as your elders tell you—
these things you dream are not possible.

    At age five, your greatest wish
was to be able to read; at six, to write a book.
And in sixth grade, when the New York author
visited your class, showed a film of his book,
you asked how you, too, could do this.
From the answers he gave, clearly, only he,
anointed and from elsewhere, could. Later,
shamefacedly trying to read his work,
you didn't enjoy it, and found it all bewildering.
(Someday you will see this book again and realize
it is poorly written – but) You were left then
believing that wishes

are like soap bubbles which lose their rainbow shine,
thin, show a gunmetal patch before they pop,
that when soap bubbles rise,
the crowd *oohs* and *aahs*—but when they disappear,
they mean nothing.

    Out in the big world you will march for rights
of people you were taught to despise. You will fight
for your own intelligence. Your choices, though
you do not see a clear and immediate outcome,
are good ones. What has always called you
will call you onward. The time will come

when you find time gone, evaporated
like fog that rises above a creek. The way
will never be clear. The ones you love
and who will leave, will always
pull at your wishes.

    But wishes, dear one,

are actually seeds of dandelions. They float
on wind like opportunists and bloom
wherever they land, an endless
annual procession of generations until
they arrive at your door. Extravagant,
they eventually colonize.

    Remember this:
Wishes come true. Within a long life, all dreams
coalesce, and manifest as you imagine.

Women Tending

"Women have sat indoors all these millions of years, so that by this time, the very walls are permeated by their creative force, which has, indeed so overcharged the capacity of bricks and mortar that it must needs harness itself to pens and brushes and business and politics."

Virginia Woolf, *A Room of One's Own*

She remembers all the women who have sat indoors tending
fires and women who walked, carrying water jugs
on their heads; waters in placental sacs within their bodies.
Women who scooped clay and breathed life into vessels,
into stories, into songs, into the material of sustenance.
They, like she, planted seeds, harvested blossoms, fruits,
roots, and seasoned meals at their tables with stories
of women through generations—the walls
permeated by the creative forces of women, the bricks
charged with dreams, suffused with memories of sunlight, rivers,
clay.

     The brick maker scoops clay from the bed of river.
     Its coolness coats her hands as she smoothes clay
     into form, evens exposed surfaces with trowel.
     At her kiln altar she kindles flame, bakes
     away water, crystals. Basalts of ocean floor
     and granites of land comingle, sing,
     and in the final flash of inferno, fuse.

     For days the bricks breathe out heat.
     They inhale sunshine, desert
     night air. The brick maker sweeps away ash.
     She lifts her bricks. One by one,
     she carries them to her secret place

by the river. One by one she massages them
with mortar, humming a Mixolydian memory
as she works. Brick by brick
she builds her place, a base as ancient
as sea floor and continent whose crystals
give rise to light and life.

  Memories of mineral pulse
  a scintillating song.

The brick maker sings
as worlds burn within her,

    The tender of the hearth
    hums as her hands push into dough,
    as she pushes another stick
    into the cooking fire

as worlds effervesce

    she hums—orients toward
    door, toward sun, leans out,
    tending toward light. She

    rises, crosses threshold
    to seek her place
    among rocks,
    at a shore,
    in a cave, beside
    a stream, within
    a light-filled room—

to set cadence to page.
She must raise herself to this task
even if no one
ever reads her words because
the great machinery of the world
depends upon
the highly-tuned listener:
the woman
who sets down her
bricks

and begins

the rendering.

Smock

Beneath the red smock she wore like a gown
two hearts beat. Hidden. Only she could say
what secret she carried to that far town.

Eighteen, alone, she moved toward the unknown,
her child, concealed, growing in her each day
beneath the red smock she wore like a gown.

Sapphire eyes blazed, she wore love like a crown;
danced with abandon at the prom in May.
Then away she slipped to the college town.

Thanksgiving, home, brothers teased how she'd grown!
What had she eaten? How much did she weigh
in the big red smock she wore like a gown?

She knew that we reap whatever we've sown.
To Mary she genuflected and prayed
for her secret in the faraway town.

She kissed her baby, then gave her away—
a story her children never have known:
Two hearts beneath a red smock like a gown;
she left one behind in that far town.

Tightrope

If you saw that squirrel in the road,
you'd swerve. For the dog trotting on the road's shoulder,
you would pull the car over and go to the farmhouse
to let them know. You would shriek to a stop—
race to the other side of the highway ahead
of the semi to scoop up the Amish toddler
and bring her back to her plain house,
her aproned mother at the door, awakened
to catastrophe, clutching her knuckles to her mouth
before taking her child back into her arms.
One breath before the world ends,
the tears fall this side of disaster
as we each place one foot in front of the other,
heels to toe, feeling the wire, its sway so high
above the crowd on the streets so far below,
holding its breath.
You weep for the father, who, beneath
the overturned canoe on the placid river moments
after paddling over the unseen dam, loses control, dives,
pulls his teenaged daughter from the waterfalls'
drowning cycle. The father lifts his daughter up before
letting go. She lives; he goes under.
You mourn the mother who threw herself
over her two-year-old child
beneath the approaching wheels
of the school bus on your city's streets,
and you walk along those streets each day
as we each put one foot in front of the other,
feel the wire, but plod with a measure of grace, try
to find a way around—

swerve—
        turn aside disaster.

A Parallelogram

consists of two lines equidistant.
We are spectator and observed, reflected
in each other's eyes. When you wake, I sleep beneath
skies charted in an ever-expanding universe
on a globe of lines and crossings,
and I wonder what grid I must cross to reach you
in Iraq, Afghanistan, Syria—or at which degree of longing
your heart beats. The world is divided,
the sky, a satellite net of impulses. But stars
still shine like diamonds. I could tell you that winter here
is cold and gray, and you could say
that sand is brown—but it's not.
In each crystal of silica
or frozen drop of water: prisms lie within.
We are composed of rainbows
arching across horizons, reaching
beyond rectangles and maps.

Come to my desert. We could wait for melt,
share cups of mint tea, and recall:
all lines are imaginary—all geometry, all plans,
just ideas. Look instead

to the trees. Like rivers, like our capillaries,
they root and branch, knitting the heart
of light and dark into curves
of longing.

Restoration

A silver earring, impressed with panic grass,
crafted by the prairie conservationist's granddaughter,
one half of a bookmatched pair,
its mirrored self a celebration
of miraculous—seed multiplied
from the restored tallgrass prairie:

lost—
like so many things in our lives, but it left my heart
broken for years, until, like a lantern in a distant, dark field,
illumination appears—all those things lost;
    gone but not forgotten:

my childhood friend, a lumpy stuffed cat, pink and limp
(for whom I was not allowed to speak my love) I last saw
carted to the curb in an ash can;

the names of childhood friends;
bullies and their power over me;
failed grades and tests with all the facts they held;

the dialect of my German relatives,
their letters sent between two world wars;
their address in the old country.

Intangible losses come into view, rise
like successive blooms in a wide prairie
releasing their sun-hungry hearts to seed, wind, time:

fears of surviving another year
in an Appalachian coal valley wracked
by depression, unemployment, cancer;
the uncertain newness of going forth in the world;
the solitary, desperate mornings;
the longing to find a home and make a family.
Ah, but when the strangely lovely family blossomed,
there was shattering. So simple a thing.
A holiday tree ornament, green,
lantern-shaped, that my mama gave to me for keeping,
the one she loved best, dropped
from the hands of my over-curious seven-year-old.

And though years later the ornament was not forgotten
by either of us, when the finely-wrought glass lay
in silver fragments on the tile floor
releasing its emptiness, it took away all brokenness
and jagged fear. The clarity

of that which was lost was reflected
in remembered silver:
the earring impressed with prairie grass,
its remaining lonely mate given away as I claimed
the power of memory and story to see each season
rise from ash, then bloom again.

Mapping the Empty Lot

where my grandmother's house stood
is like tonguing a lost tooth. I cannot
find my bearings. Only broken boulevard flagstones say
there was a home here once.
Gravel replaces grassy yard.
I am at a loss
to restore the snapdragon-lined passage
from hedge in front
to where apple trees blossomed in back; the place
along the fence where we children scavenged
pears and plums from the old lady next door
who yelled whenever we got near.
I pace the ghost house
where barrels of apple wine once
convened in the basement and jam jars dribbled
sweetness along wooden shelves, while upstairs
at the dining room table, we gathered
for Thanksgiving.
I strip veneer
from memory and try to measure
the gap in years, all that happened
in this place: the fears for sons
gone to war, the path worn from mailbox to door.
Their mother prayed over photos of them in uniform
on the living room wall while she waited
to caress their faces. The sons
returned from their hidden hells
emptied, their souls scattered, shattered
by mortars. Time moved on
without them, as the shells of their lives filled the halls.

My grandmother sat
in the rocking chair, swaying
back and forth
on her crumbling front porch floor
where she still hovers.
And I, on empty gravel, still search
for the door.

What Remains

The mother in her aproned plissé dress on linoleum,
the father, asleep on the couch after another shift
at the fire station, the Lionel trains buzzing
and clicking on their three-rail track, the brother
at the lever watching it all run, run, run
in endless loops of lemiscate.
The lone surviving spruce tree planted for Arbor Day,
this one from kindergarten, still grows fluffy and low,
and the orange tabby still places his paws across
the gray-painted porch with heavy precision.
The swingset painted a weary barn-red waits for you
to fly, the tiny cherry tree planted by your hands
from a pit along with the peach seedling reaches for the sky.
All of it remains: the vivid aqua blue pool
at the city playground down the street and all of the feet
splashing through its slapping, draining waters
each ending of a summer day.
This, too, stays and does not melt away:
wet snow in heaps over ash cans, piles
of neighbor kids flying on sleds downhill
on a never-ending snow day away from school,
the way navy blue wool hats and scarves
and knitted red mittens cook on silver radiators
when face-cold and satisfied,
we arrive in time to go indoors for soup and bed.

All of it still lives: grandmas with crumpled tissues stuffed
at their bosoms, their hugs, warm and papery-crinkled,
and tea at the enamel kitchen table with them
and their wispy gray-haired old lady friends,
the beers at taverns with the men
and shot-glass colas through needlelike cocktail straws
while the jukebox belts out blues.

Coal trains still chug,
smoke rises in the mining valley,
cinders on snow turn it a sad yellow,
wispy blue flames cover mountains
of burning coal waste at night,
while in daylight the many-colored sparks
flash on burning culm mountains as raindrops strike.

Still there rests
the grace of June in deep green mountain woods
and the startling joy of holiday tree lights
red-green-ocher-blue at year's end reflected
from each strand of tinsel, each fluted indent
of each silvery moment.

All of it, all here. All time remains.

Recollection

It's the same route each time I visit the antique shop:
round the Depression glass ruby and rose,
the lace-edged doilies draped over
oak-veneered dressers and veer
to white enamel kettles rimmed in black,
complete with balers. I don't know how
I would use them, but wish to rescue them
from mishandling. I pass linens,
piles of square tablecloths meant for unblemished
porcelain-topped family kitchen tables.
I saunter to aprons and search
for McCoy pottery, the real thing, striped pink and blue,
hoping for the spouted mixing bowl I gave up
at a hardware store thirty years ago
and still regret. I move on to empty canning jars,
sold at antique store prices.

I want to tell you there, behind the counter
with your dangly earrings and chic apparel,
you, with your clever auction bids: I seek
blue Ball jars I'll fill with produce and preserve
a generation's dignity. Shouldn't there be special prices
for those of us who hold traditions,
having used these tools continuously
for half a century? We are keepers
of memory. We sift our flour, ream
our lemons on green glass, mash potatoes
with wooden-handled deftness.
We saw the Depression through
our parents, who filled jars
with Victory Garden fervor
and sealed them in steaming kettles
against the onslaught of time.

Revolution

When I'm gone
all that I tried to control
will run wild, and with it,
all that I tried not to control.
At each doorstep, orange lilies.
Tulips will cavort with the garlic,
which, cloning itself many times over,
will overspread the yard.
Fruit trees and shrubs will succor bees;
dangle shriveled apples and berries.
Flocks will feast then rise
as foxes prowl beneath
sprawling brambles.
I know this
even as I plant yet more bulbs,
set trees into a compost-filled trench;
deer will browse these at leisure.
I will roll over
in my crypt of soil and ash.
My wild Eden once regained,
will evolve; I will turn over
endlessly to blossom.

Matter

Matter, I've been told, cannot be created or destroyed—

and still I wonder what comes after this life of breakage
and strain. If I could send an emissary to an afterlife,
would she return saying:

It's grand! Full of swan boats and magnificent music,

or

*It's simply too dark to describe—less light comes through
than in a mile-deep mine.*   For me

annihilation would be fine. No need for worry if matter
transforms from molecule to galaxy,
or particles change partners to the atom's pulse.
The tiniest specks that comprise each stone and being
once swirled in ancient seas,
drifted downward,
made their bed in sediment on ocean floor.
The flesh and bone of which we are made,
compressed into stone:
uplifted;
eroded;
dissolved;
floated;
coalesced, to plunge again,
amphibious this time, through placental waters—
only momentarily breaking free—
from ocean.

Panoramic

From the view of this precious age,
as landscape seen from an eagle's lair,
the lay of life is good, fulfilled.
Every heartbeat,
each purr the ears have known, every
day whose light is scattered
by clouds of every color
is a goblet brim-full
of rainbow, complemented
with sparks and darkness both.
In the course of eons
black coal transforms, hardens
to diamond reflecting each hue,
tint and tone; the palette brings
multifaceted vision.
Beyond this moment,
this life, I wish to see

how bees follow ley lines
to the center, ovary deep,
then out again winging,
warmed by solar rays
to follow paths scented
with others' passings
in the buzz-filled air.

Passerine

When my time is over, if I were to choose,
(I've told my children,)
in the next life I would be

a swallow,
swoop from sky to ground,
scoop mud up in my beak
to place on the barn rafter. I'd build
a shallow shelf, a dish nest of dry adobe,
a token of loyalty to my family—
not to last forever after, but to hold on only
as long as the life will last in the barn:
shelter for so very unseen many.

And on the shelf, I would keep my nestlings, sweep
the air for food to feed my beak-open young,
show them, when fledging, how to leap
and trust air to hold their future—

and leave at the golden fat-blooming season
of sunflower, fly far, find adventure,
sail home in spring on waves of apple blossom
and first sweet clover—

—I'd choose swallow when my time is over.

Geosmin Notes

"Stone Circle"

Inspired by a painted image of Castlerigg Stone Circle in Cumbria U.K. by Catherine Edmund.

"While your glass spectacles / dissolve into puddles" refers to glass as a slow liquid that pools over time.

"Eloquence Engraved in Stone"

Tony Hoagland's poem "Description" prompted an ekphrastic response describing the limestone and sandstone bluffs that line the Upper Mississippi River which geologists interpret as deposits from ancient seas and beaches.

"Color of Water"

"blood-borne / *incarnadine* / chlorophyll-laden / *verdant*"

But for the central element in the molecular structure of chlorophyll and blood (magnesium and iron, respectively) the waters that run through all living beings are very much the same.

"At A Loss"

Migizi is the Anishinaabemowin word for bald eagle. *Migizi* flies at dawn to see if humans remember to greet the day so that the world may continue.

"Stippled Passing"

Responds to Gerard Manley Hopkins' poem, "Pied Beauty" with its line: "For rose-moles all stipple upon trout that swim."

"The Ripening Abcedarian"

"zymurgy" here refers to fermentation.

"Invocation: Call It Home"

This poem was first published as a poster designed by artist Stephanie Motz.

"What I Love about Where I Live, Driftless Region"

Driftless refers to the rugged, unglaciated bioregion in the upper Midwest encasing the Mississippi River. An anomaly in the North American continent, it is a fragile, biodiverse environment of sandstone and limestone-layered hills and hollows carved by numerous springwater creeks. It is a rich agricultural land threatened of depopulation, thoughtless construction, and frack sand mining.

"When Freshly Painted"

The poem is an ekphrastic response to Marion Clarke's bucolic painting *Chickens!* depicting a flock of hens and a rooster in front of thatched-roofed, whitewashed cottage with doors painted bright red.

"A Parallelogram"

A response to the photograph "Met" by Dave Thewlis in which echoes and reflections of window panels frame a snowy landscape.

"Passerine"

A passerine is a perching songbird in the avian order Passeriformes, which includes swallows.

Acknowledgements

The author gratefully acknowledges the periodicals in which these poems first appeared:

Ascent: "Firefly Nights"

About Place: "Women Tending"

Aqueous: "Minus Forty", "Shoreline Instructions for Lake Superior"

Camas: "Lost at Sea"

Cold Mountain Review: "Gathering Acorns, Hoarding Words"

Common Ground Review: "Superior", "Waters Silvered"

Flyway: "July 4", "Farmer / Janus"

Fourth River: "Stone Circle"

Freshwater: "Mapping the Empty Lot"

Literary Mama: "Smock"

Minding Nature: "At a Loss"

Passager: "Panoramic"

Reliquiae: "Hymenoptera I: Wasps", "Verdancy"

River Heron: "A Parallelogram", "Stippled Passing"

Tiny Seed Journal: "In Dark Times We Gather Light"

Wisconsin Review: "Volute"

Additional Acknowledgements

"Art Goes Unbidden" and "Barn Elegiac" were published in the anthology *Contours: A Literary Landscape*, by Driftless Writing Center.

"Gathering Acorns, Hoarding Words" received Reader's Choice Award from *Cold Mountain Review*.

"A Parallelogram" was nominated for a Pushcart Prize.

I am grateful for the support of Write On Door County in offering time and space for the writing and revision of these poems, and for their workshops.

Thank you to the generous people in my writing groups for their deep consideration of my work; for Linda Lieb, my cohort in creativity; for my family members who patiently listen to each iteration of everything I write.

Catherine Young is a writer and performing artist whose work is infused with a keen sense of place. She worked as a national park ranger, educator, farmer, and mother before putting her heart into her writing. Her prose and ecopoetry is published internationally and nationally, and her writing has been nominated for the Pushcart Prize and Best American Essays. Catherine holds an MFA from the University of British Columbia. Rooted in farm life, Catherine lives with her family in Wisconsin's Driftless bioregion where she is totally in love with meandering streams.

For more visit:
www.catherineyoungwriter.com

Photography by Celeste Thalhammer

CPSIA information can be obtained
at www.ICGtesting.com
Printed in the USA
LVHW040940311221
707391LV00007B/30/J